EMMANUEL JOSEPH

The Legacy Code, Cracking the Secrets of Billionaire Influence and Immortality

*Copyright © 2025 by Emmanuel Joseph*

*All rights reserved. No part of this publication may be reproduced, stored or transmitted in any form or by any means, electronic, mechanical, photocopying, recording, scanning, or otherwise without written permission from the publisher. It is illegal to copy this book, post it to a website, or distribute it by any other means without permission.*

*First edition*

*This book was professionally typeset on Reedsy. Find out more at reedsy.com*

# Contents

| | | |
|---|---|---|
| 1 | Chapter 1: The Genesis of Wealth | 1 |
| 2 | Chapter 2: The Power of Vision | 3 |
| 3 | Chapter 3: The Influence of Networks | 5 |
| 4 | Chapter 4: The Art of Deal-Making | 7 |
| 5 | Chapter 5: The Pursuit of Innovation | 9 |
| 6 | Chapter 6: The Psychology of Risk | 11 |
| 7 | Chapter 7: The Power of Branding | 13 |
| 8 | Chapter 8: The Role of Philanthropy | 15 |
| 9 | Chapter 9: The Power of Media | 17 |
| 10 | Chapter 10: The Importance of Legacy Planning | 19 |
| 11 | Chapter 11: The Science of Longevity | 21 |
| 12 | Chapter 12: The Role of Education | 23 |
| 13 | Chapter 13: The Impact of Technology | 25 |
| 14 | Chapter 14: The Power of Resilience | 27 |
| 15 | Chapter 15: The Ethics of Wealth | 29 |
| 16 | Chapter 16: The Global Impact | 31 |
| 17 | Chapter 17: The Future of Billionaire Influence | 33 |

# 1

# Chapter 1: The Genesis of Wealth

From the lush valleys of Silicon Valley to the towering skyscrapers of Wall Street, the birthplaces of the world's wealthiest individuals are as varied as their paths to success. They are the modern-day alchemists, turning ideas into gold and forging empires from the ethereal realms of technology and finance. Their journeys often start with a spark of innovation, a glimpse into the future that others cannot see. But what is the true essence that transforms a mere mortal into a billionaire? Is it pure genius, relentless drive, or simply being at the right place at the right time? In this opening chapter, we delve into the origins of wealth, exploring the backgrounds, early influences, and pivotal moments that set these titans on their paths to unprecedented riches.

The story of each billionaire begins with a unique blend of personal ambition and external circumstances. Some are born into privilege, with access to education and opportunities that pave the way for their ascent. Others rise from humble beginnings, driven by a fierce determination to change their destinies. Regardless of their starting points, these individuals share a common trait: an unwavering belief in their visions. This belief propels them forward, even in the face of adversity, and fuels their relentless pursuit of success.

In the early stages of their journeys, many billionaires encounter pivotal moments that shape their futures. These moments often come in the form of opportunities disguised as challenges. A struggling startup, a failed project, or a seemingly insurmountable obstacle can become the catalyst for innovation and growth. The ability to recognize and seize these opportunities is a hallmark of the billionaire mindset. It is this mindset that allows them to turn setbacks into stepping stones, transforming potential failure into extraordinary success.

As they navigate the complex landscape of business and finance, billionaires are guided by a unique combination of skills and qualities. Visionary thinking, strategic decision-making, and an innate understanding of market dynamics are all essential components of their success. But beyond these technical skills, there is something more intangible: a sense of purpose that drives them to create and build. This purpose is often rooted in a desire to make a lasting impact on the world, to leave a legacy that extends beyond their personal achievements.

# 2

# Chapter 2: The Power of Vision

Vision is the cornerstone of every great fortune. Billionaires possess a unique ability to envision the world not as it is, but as it could be. This chapter unravels the minds of these visionaries, examining how they identify opportunities, anticipate market shifts, and make bold decisions that others fear to contemplate. From Elon Musk's interplanetary ambitions to Jeff Bezos' relentless pursuit of a customer-centric universe, we dissect the ingredients that fuel their audacious visions. How do they stay ahead of the curve? What mental frameworks guide their thinking? The answers lie in a combination of foresight, adaptability, and a relentless pursuit of their dreams.

For these visionaries, the future is a canvas waiting to be painted with their ideas. They see opportunities where others see obstacles, and they possess the courage to pursue their dreams, even when the path is fraught with uncertainty. This chapter delves into the cognitive processes that enable billionaires to anticipate trends and make strategic decisions. We explore how they cultivate a mindset of continuous learning and adaptability, allowing them to pivot and innovate in response to changing circumstances.

One key aspect of their vision is the ability to think long-term. While many are focused on short-term gains, billionaires often have a broader perspective, looking decades into the future. This long-term thinking enables them to make investments and take risks that others might shy away from.

We examine the role of patience, perseverance, and strategic planning in their journey to success. By understanding the importance of long-term vision, we gain insight into how billionaires build and sustain their empires.

Moreover, vision is not just about seeing the future; it's about creating it. Billionaires are not passive observers; they are active participants in shaping the world around them. This chapter highlights the importance of taking bold action, experimenting with new ideas, and challenging the status quo. Through the stories of visionary leaders like Elon Musk and Jeff Bezos, we uncover the principles and practices that drive their transformative visions.

# 3

# Chapter 3: The Influence of Networks

No billionaire stands alone. Behind every great fortune is a network of relationships that spans the globe. In this chapter, we explore the intricate web of connections that amplify the influence of these financial titans. From strategic partnerships and alliances to mentorship and philanthropic endeavors, we uncover how billionaires leverage their networks to expand their reach and solidify their legacies. What role do personal and professional relationships play in their success? How do they navigate the delicate balance of power, trust, and loyalty? The power of networks is a critical component in the legacy code of billionaires, and understanding it is key to unlocking their secrets.

Billionaires understand that their success is not solely the result of individual effort; it is also the product of collaboration and support from others. This chapter delves into the importance of building and nurturing relationships, both personal and professional. We explore how billionaires cultivate networks that provide access to resources, opportunities, and expertise. These networks are often built over time, through a combination of trust, reciprocity, and mutual benefit.

Strategic partnerships play a crucial role in the success of billionaires. By forming alliances with other influential individuals and organizations, they can amplify their impact and achieve their goals more efficiently. This chapter examines how billionaires identify and cultivate strategic partnerships, and how they navigate the complexities of these relationships. We also explore the role of mentorship, both as mentors and mentees, in their journey to success.

Philanthropy is another important aspect of billionaire networks. By giving back to their communities and supporting causes they care about, billionaires not only make a positive impact on the world but also strengthen their networks. This chapter highlights the ways in which philanthropy enhances their influence and legacy. By understanding the importance of networks, we gain insight into the collaborative nature of billionaire success.

# 4

# Chapter 4: The Art of Deal-Making

Deals are the lifeblood of billionaire fortunes. Whether it's a high-stakes acquisition, a groundbreaking merger, or a savvy investment, the ability to craft and execute deals sets billionaires apart. This chapter delves into the art and science of deal-making, examining the strategies, negotiations, and instincts that drive these financial powerhouses. How do they identify lucrative opportunities? What tactics do they employ to close deals? From Warren Buffett's value investing to the aggressive tactics of corporate raiders, we explore the diverse approaches that billionaires use to amass and protect their wealth.

Deal-making is a complex and multifaceted process that requires a combination of analytical skills, intuition, and strategic thinking. This chapter explores the key elements of successful deal-making, from identifying opportunities to negotiating terms and closing the deal. We examine the role of due diligence, risk assessment, and financial analysis in the deal-making process. By understanding these elements, we gain insight into how billionaires make informed decisions that maximize their returns.

Negotiation is a critical aspect of deal-making, and billionaires are often master negotiators. This chapter delves into the strategies and tactics they use to achieve favorable outcomes. We explore the importance of preparation, effective communication, and flexibility in negotiations. By studying the negotiation styles of successful deal-makers like Warren Buffett, we gain valuable lessons in the art of negotiation.

Furthermore, deal-making is not just about acquiring assets; it's also about creating value. Billionaires are skilled at identifying opportunities to add value through strategic investments, operational improvements, and innovative business models. This chapter highlights the importance of value creation in the deal-making process. By understanding how billionaires create value, we gain insight into their ability to build and grow successful enterprises.

# 5

# Chapter 5: The Pursuit of Innovation

Innovation is the engine of economic growth and a hallmark of billionaire influence. In this chapter, we examine how the world's wealthiest individuals drive innovation within their industries and beyond. What fuels their desire to push the boundaries of what's possible? How do they cultivate a culture of innovation within their organizations? From the technological breakthroughs of Bill Gates and Steve Jobs to the disruptive business models of Airbnb and Uber, we explore the relentless pursuit of innovation that defines the billionaire mindset. Innovation is not just about creating new products or services; it's about reshaping entire industries and rewriting the rules of the game.

The pursuit of innovation is a defining characteristic of billionaires, and it often begins with a mindset of curiosity and creativity. This chapter delves into the cognitive processes that drive innovation, from generating new ideas to experimenting with different approaches. We explore how billionaires foster a culture of innovation within their organizations, encouraging their teams to think outside the box and embrace risk-taking.

Technological advancements are a key driver of innovation, and billionaires are often at the forefront of technological change. This chapter examines the role of technology in their success, from the development of groundbreaking products to the implementation of cutting-edge business models. We explore the ways in which billionaires leverage technology to disrupt industries and create new markets.

Moreover, innovation is not just about technology; it's also about business strategy. Billionaires are skilled at identifying and capitalizing on emerging trends, and they often employ innovative business models to gain a competitive edge. This chapter highlights the importance of strategic thinking in the pursuit of innovation. By understanding the strategic approaches of successful innovators like Bill Gates and Steve Jobs, we gain valuable insights into the mindset and practices that drive their success.

# 6

# Chapter 6: The Psychology of Risk

Risk-taking is an inherent part of the journey to billionaire status. But what separates the calculated risk-taker from the reckless gambler? In this chapter, we delve into the psychology of risk, exploring how billionaires assess and manage uncertainty. What mental frameworks guide their decision-making processes? How do they balance the potential rewards against the inherent dangers? From the high-stakes world of venture capital to the volatile terrain of emerging markets, we uncover the strategies and mindsets that enable billionaires to navigate risk with confidence and precision.

Risk-taking requires a deep understanding of the factors at play and the ability to weigh potential outcomes. Billionaires often employ a combination of analytical thinking and intuition to assess risks. This chapter examines the tools and techniques they use to evaluate risk, including financial models, scenario planning, and stress testing. We also explore the role of intuition in their decision-making processes. How do they develop and trust their instincts? What role does experience play in honing their intuition?

Moreover, billionaires are skilled at managing risk. They understand that risk cannot be eliminated, but it can be mitigated. This chapter highlights the strategies they use to manage and reduce risk, from diversification and hedging to insurance and contingency planning. We also examine the importance of resilience and adaptability in navigating risk. How do billionaires respond to unexpected challenges and setbacks? What mental and emotional tools do they rely on to stay resilient in the face of adversity?

Ultimately, the psychology of risk is about finding the right balance between caution and boldness. This chapter explores the delicate balance that billionaires strike in their pursuit of success. By understanding their approach to risk, we gain valuable insights into the mindset and practices that enable them to achieve extraordinary results.

# 7

# Chapter 7: The Power of Branding

A strong personal and corporate brand is a powerful asset in the arsenal of billionaires. This chapter explores how the world's wealthiest individuals cultivate and leverage their brands to enhance their influence and extend their reach. What are the key elements of a successful brand? How do billionaires use branding to shape public perception and build loyal followings? From the iconic apple of Steve Jobs to the electric charisma of Richard Branson, we examine the role of branding in the legacy code of billionaire success. A well-crafted brand not only drives business success but also creates a lasting impact on the world.

Branding is more than just a logo or a tagline; it is the essence of what a company or individual stands for. This chapter delves into the elements that make up a successful brand, from core values and mission statements to visual identity and customer experience. We explore how billionaires define and articulate their brand values, and how they ensure consistency across all touchpoints. By understanding the key elements of branding, we gain insight into how billionaires create and maintain strong brands.

One of the most important aspects of branding is authenticity. Billionaires understand that authenticity is key to building trust and loyalty. This chapter examines how billionaires stay true to their brand values and maintain authenticity in their actions and communications. We also explore the role of storytelling in branding. How do billionaires use stories to connect with their audiences and convey their brand values? What role does narrative play in building a strong brand?

Moreover, branding is an ongoing process. Billionaires are constantly evolving and adapting their brands to stay relevant in a changing world. This chapter highlights the importance of staying attuned to market trends and customer needs. By understanding how billionaires adapt and innovate their brands, we gain valuable insights into the practices that drive long-term brand success.

# 8

# Chapter 8: The Role of Philanthropy

Philanthropy is more than just a moral obligation; it's a strategic tool for billionaires to cement their legacies and shape the future. In this chapter, we explore the philanthropic endeavors of the world's wealthiest individuals, examining the motivations, strategies, and impact of their giving. How do they choose the causes they support? What role does philanthropy play in their overall legacy? From the transformative initiatives of the Gates Foundation to the innovative approaches of the Chan Zuckerberg Initiative, we uncover the ways in which billionaires use their wealth to address some of the world's most pressing challenges.

Philanthropy allows billionaires to make a positive impact on society and contribute to the greater good. This chapter delves into the motivations behind their philanthropic efforts, from personal values and passions to strategic goals and public relations. We explore how billionaires identify and select the causes they support, and how they align their philanthropic efforts with their overall vision and mission. By understanding their motivations, we gain insight into the driving forces behind their giving.

Moreover, philanthropy is not just about giving money; it's about creating meaningful change. This chapter examines the strategies and approaches billionaires use to maximize the impact of their philanthropy. From targeted grants and investments to innovative partnerships and collaborative initiatives, we explore the ways in which billionaires leverage their resources to drive social and environmental progress. We also highlight the importance of measurement and evaluation in philanthropy. How do billionaires assess the effectiveness of their efforts? What role does impact measurement play in their decision-making processes?

Furthermore, philanthropy enhances the influence and legacy of billionaires. By addressing critical issues and supporting transformative initiatives, billionaires not only make a positive impact on the world but also strengthen their networks and build their reputations. This chapter highlights the ways in which philanthropy contributes to the long-term success and legacy of billionaires. By understanding the role of philanthropy in their lives, we gain valuable insights into their holistic approach to wealth and influence.

# 9

## Chapter 9: The Power of Media

In an age of information overload, controlling the narrative is a key aspect of billionaire influence. This chapter delves into the relationship between billionaires and the media, exploring how they use traditional and digital platforms to shape public opinion and advance their agendas. How do billionaires manage their public personas? What strategies do they use to navigate media scrutiny and maintain a positive image? From the media empires of Rupert Murdoch to the social media prowess of Elon Musk, we examine the ways in which billionaires harness the power of media to amplify their influence and achieve their goals.

The media is a powerful tool for shaping public perception and influencing opinions. This chapter explores how billionaires use media to build their brands, communicate their messages, and engage with their audiences. We examine the role of traditional media, such as newspapers, television, and radio, as well as the growing influence of digital media, including social media, blogs, and podcasts. By understanding the diverse media landscape, we gain insight into how billionaires navigate and leverage different platforms.

One of the most important aspects of media strategy is controlling the narrative. Billionaires understand the importance of managing their public personas and shaping the stories that are told about them. This chapter delves into the techniques and tactics they use to control the narrative, from media training and strategic communications to crisis management and reputation management. We explore the role of transparency, authenticity, and storytelling in building and maintaining a positive image.

Moreover, billionaires are skilled at using media to advance their agendas and achieve their goals. This chapter highlights the ways in which billionaires use media to influence public opinion, drive policy change, and promote their initiatives. We examine the role of media campaigns, public relations efforts, and advocacy in their media strategies. By understanding how billionaires leverage the power of media, we gain valuable insights into their ability to shape the world around them.

# 10

# Chapter 10: The Importance of Legacy Planning

Legacy planning is a critical aspect of the billionaire mindset. This chapter explores how the world's wealthiest individuals think about and prepare for the future, ensuring that their influence and impact endure beyond their lifetimes. What strategies do they use to safeguard their wealth and pass it on to future generations? How do they balance personal and philanthropic goals in their legacy planning? From the establishment of family trusts to the creation of charitable foundations, we uncover the various approaches billionaires use to leave a lasting legacy that reflects their values and vision.

Legacy planning involves a combination of financial strategies, legal structures, and personal values. This chapter delves into the tools and techniques billionaires use to create and protect their legacies. We explore the role of trusts, wills, and estate planning in ensuring the smooth transfer of wealth to future generations. By understanding these tools, we gain insight into how billionaires safeguard their fortunes and ensure their continued influence.

One important aspect of legacy planning is the alignment of personal and philanthropic goals. Billionaires often use their wealth to support causes they care about, creating a lasting impact on society. This chapter examines how billionaires integrate philanthropy into their legacy planning, from the creation of charitable foundations to the establishment of donor-advised funds. We explore the motivations behind their giving and the ways in which they ensure their philanthropic efforts align with their overall vision and values.

Furthermore, legacy planning is not just about financial wealth; it is also about values, knowledge, and influence. This chapter highlights the importance of passing on these intangible assets to future generations. We explore the ways in which billionaires mentor and educate their heirs, ensuring they are equipped to carry on their legacies. By understanding the holistic approach to legacy planning, we gain valuable insights into the practices that enable billionaires to create enduring impact.

# 11

## Chapter 11: The Science of Longevity

The quest for immortality has long fascinated humanity, and billionaires are no exception. This chapter delves into the scientific and technological advancements that billionaires are investing in to extend their lifespans and enhance their quality of life. What breakthroughs are on the horizon in the fields of biotechnology, genetics, and artificial intelligence? How do billionaires balance the desire for longevity with the ethical implications of these advancements? From the futuristic visions of Peter Thiel to the cutting-edge research of Google's Calico, we explore the intersection of wealth, science, and the pursuit of immortality.

Advancements in biotechnology and genetics are opening new possibilities for extending human life. This chapter examines the latest research and innovations in these fields, from gene editing and regenerative medicine to anti-aging therapies and personalized medicine. We explore how billionaires are funding and supporting these advancements, and how they are incorporating them into their own lives. By understanding the science of longevity, we gain insight into the future of health and wellness.

Artificial intelligence is another area of interest for billionaires in their quest for longevity. This chapter delves into the ways in which AI is being used to enhance healthcare, from early disease detection and diagnosis to personalized treatment plans and robotic surgery. We explore the potential of AI to revolutionize healthcare and extend human lifespans.

By understanding the role of AI in longevity, we gain insight into the technological advancements that are shaping the future.

Moreover, the pursuit of longevity raises important ethical considerations. This chapter examines the ethical implications of extending human life, from issues of accessibility and inequality to the potential impact on society and the environment. We explore how billionaires navigate these ethical dilemmas and balance their desire for longevity with their commitment to ethical principles. By understanding the ethical considerations of longevity, we gain valuable insights into the complexities of this pursuit.

## 12

## Chapter 12: The Role of Education

Education is a powerful tool for empowerment and influence. In this chapter, we examine how billionaires invest in education, both for themselves and for others, to drive innovation and create opportunities. How do they prioritize learning and skill development throughout their lives? What impact do their educational initiatives have on society? From the pioneering efforts of Andrew Carnegie to the modern-day investments of Mark Zuckerberg, we uncover the ways in which education plays a central role in the legacy code of billionaire success.

Continuous learning is a hallmark of the billionaire mindset. This chapter delves into the importance of lifelong learning and skill development for billionaires. We explore how they prioritize education and stay ahead of the curve in a rapidly changing world. From executive education programs to online courses and mentorship, we examine the various ways in which billionaires invest in their own learning and growth.

Billionaires also invest in education for others, recognizing its power to create opportunities and drive social change. This chapter highlights the educational initiatives and philanthropic efforts of billionaires, from scholarships and grants to school building projects and educational technology. We explore the impact of these initiatives on individuals and communities, and how they contribute to the broader goals of economic development and social progress.

Moreover, education is not just about formal learning; it is also about cultivating a mindset of curiosity and innovation. This chapter examines how billionaires foster a culture of curiosity and innovation within their organizations and communities. By understanding the role of education in their lives, we gain valuable insights into the practices that drive their success and influence.

# 13

# Chapter 13: The Impact of Technology

Technology is a driving force behind the fortunes of many billionaires. This chapter explores how technological advancements shape their businesses, investments, and influence. What are the key trends and innovations that billionaires are betting on? How do they navigate the ever-changing landscape of the tech industry? From the rise of artificial intelligence to the promise of blockchain, we examine the technological forces that are redefining the future and the strategies billionaires use to stay ahead of the curve.

Technological innovation is a key driver of economic growth and a source of competitive advantage for billionaires. This chapter delves into the latest trends and developments in the tech industry, from AI and machine learning to blockchain and quantum computing. We explore how billionaires identify and invest in these emerging technologies, and how they leverage them to create new business opportunities and disrupt existing industries.

Moreover, technology is not just about creating new products and services; it is also about transforming the way we live and work. This chapter examines the broader impact of technological advancements on society and the economy. We explore how billionaires are using technology to address global challenges, from climate change and healthcare to education and social inequality. By understanding the impact of technology, we gain valuable insights into the ways in which billionaires are shaping the future.

The tech industry is constantly evolving, and staying ahead of the curve requires a combination of foresight, adaptability, and innovation. This chapter highlights the strategies billionaires use to navigate the ever-changing landscape of technology. We explore the importance of continuous learning, strategic thinking, and collaboration in their approach to the tech industry. By understanding their strategies, we gain valuable insights into the practices that enable billionaires to thrive in a dynamic and competitive environment.

# 14

## Chapter 14: The Power of Resilience

Resilience is a defining trait of billionaires, enabling them to overcome setbacks and emerge stronger. This chapter delves into the stories of perseverance and grit that characterize their journeys. How do they navigate challenges and turn adversity into opportunity? What mental and emotional tools do they rely on to stay resilient? From the comeback stories of Steve Jobs to the relentless determination of Oprah Winfrey, we explore the resilience that underpins the success of billionaires and offers valuable lessons for anyone striving to achieve greatness.

Resilience is the ability to bounce back from adversity and continue pursuing one's goals. This chapter examines the mindset and practices that enable billionaires to stay resilient in the face of challenges. We explore the importance of maintaining a positive attitude, staying focused on long-term goals, and developing coping strategies to manage stress and setbacks. By understanding the mental and emotional tools of resilience, we gain valuable insights into the practices that drive long-term success.

One key aspect of resilience is the ability to learn from failure. Billionaires often view failure as an opportunity for growth and improvement rather than a setback. This chapter highlights the importance of adopting a growth mindset and embracing failure as a natural part of the journey. We explore the ways in which billionaires reflect on their experiences, extract valuable lessons, and use them to inform their future decisions. By understanding their approach to failure, we gain valuable insights into the practices that enable them to persevere and thrive.

Moreover, resilience is not just about individual effort; it is also about building a supportive environment. This chapter examines the role of support networks, mentorship, and collaboration in fostering resilience. We explore how billionaires leverage their relationships and resources to navigate challenges and achieve their goals. By understanding the power of resilience, we gain valuable insights into the practices that drive long-term success and influence.

# 15

# Chapter 15: The Ethics of Wealth

With great wealth comes great responsibility. In this chapter, we explore the ethical considerations and dilemmas that billionaires face as they wield their influence and resources. How do they navigate the fine line between ambition and exploitation? What role does ethical leadership play in their decision-making processes? From the controversies surrounding tech giants to the philanthropic efforts addressing global inequality, we examine the complex interplay between wealth, power, and ethics.

Ethical leadership is a critical aspect of billionaire success. This chapter delves into the principles and practices that guide their decision-making processes, from integrity and transparency to social responsibility and sustainability. We explore how billionaires balance their ambitions with their commitment to ethical principles, and how they navigate the challenges and dilemmas that arise in their pursuit of success. By understanding the importance of ethical leadership, we gain valuable insights into the practices that drive responsible and sustainable wealth creation.

Moreover, wealth comes with the power to shape society and influence public policy. This chapter examines the ethical implications of billionaire influence, from issues of inequality and social justice to the impact of their business practices on the environment and communities. We explore the ways in which billionaires use their wealth to drive positive change and address pressing global challenges. By understanding the ethical considerations of wealth, we gain valuable insights into the complexities of billionaire influence.

Furthermore, ethics is not just about individual actions; it is also about creating a culture of integrity and accountability within organizations. This chapter highlights the importance of fostering ethical cultures within businesses and institutions. We explore the role of corporate governance, ethical training, and stakeholder engagement in promoting ethical behavior. By understanding the importance of ethical cultures, we gain valuable insights into the practices that drive responsible and sustainable business practices.

# 16

# Chapter 16: The Global Impact

Billionaires have a profound impact on the global stage, shaping economies, cultures, and societies. This chapter examines the broader implications of their influence, from economic development to geopolitical dynamics. How do their decisions and actions affect the world at large? What role do billionaires play in addressing global challenges such as climate change and social inequality? From the global reach of multinational corporations to the philanthropic initiatives targeting systemic issues, we explore the far-reaching impact of billionaire influence.

Economic development is one of the most significant areas of billionaire influence. This chapter delves into the ways in which billionaires drive economic growth, from investments in emerging markets to the creation of jobs and opportunities. We explore the role of entrepreneurship, innovation, and strategic investments in fostering economic development. By understanding the economic impact of billionaires, we gain valuable insights into the ways in which they shape the global economy.

Moreover, billionaires play a crucial role in addressing global challenges. This chapter examines the ways in which they leverage their resources and influence to tackle pressing issues such as climate change, poverty, and social inequality. We explore the impact of their philanthropic efforts, from funding research and innovation to supporting grassroots initiatives and advocacy. By understanding the global impact of billionaires, we gain valuable insights into the ways in which they contribute to social and environmental progress.

Furthermore, billionaire influence extends beyond economic and social impact; it also shapes cultural and geopolitical dynamics. This chapter highlights the ways in which billionaires influence cultural trends, public opinion, and policy decisions. We explore the role of media, entertainment, and public engagement in their strategies. By understanding the global impact of billionaires, we gain valuable insights into the multifaceted nature of their influence.

# 17

## Chapter 17: The Future of Billionaire Influence

As we look to the future, the landscape of billionaire influence is poised for transformation. In this concluding chapter, we consider the emerging trends and challenges that will shape the next generation of billionaires. What opportunities and threats lie ahead? How will advances in technology, shifts in global power dynamics, and changing societal values redefine the legacy code of billionaire success? From the rise of new industries to the evolving expectations of wealth and leadership, we explore the future of billionaire influence and the lessons it holds for aspiring leaders.

The future of billionaire influence will be shaped by a combination of technological advancements, economic shifts, and societal changes. This chapter delves into the key trends and developments that will define the next generation of billionaires, from the rise of artificial intelligence and automation to the growth of sustainable and impact investing. We explore the opportunities and challenges that these trends present, and how billionaires are positioning themselves to navigate and capitalize on them.

Moreover, the future of billionaire influence will be defined by changing expectations of wealth and leadership. This chapter examines the evolving role of billionaires in society, from ethical and responsible leadership to inclusive and equitable wealth distribution. We explore the ways in which societal values and expectations are shaping the future of billionaire influence, and how aspiring leaders can align their goals with these values. By understanding the future of billionaire influence, we gain valuable insights into the practices that will drive long-term success and impact.

Furthermore, the future of billionaire influence will be characterized by greater collaboration and global interconnectedness. This chapter highlights the importance of building and nurturing networks, partnerships, and alliances to address global challenges and create sustainable solutions. We explore the role of collaboration in driving innovation, economic development, and social progress. By understanding the future of billionaire influence, we gain valuable insights into the practices that will shape the next generation of leaders and change-makers.

**The Legacy Code: Cracking the Secrets of Billionaire Influence and Immortality**

In "The Legacy Code: Cracking the Secrets of Billionaire Influence and Immortality," delve into the minds and strategies of the world's wealthiest individuals. This insightful and meticulously researched book unravels the secrets behind the unprecedented success, enduring influence, and quests for immortality of billionaires.

From the birthplaces of wealth to the intricate art of deal-making, the book explores the multifaceted elements that shape billionaire fortunes. Discover how visionary thinking, strategic networking, and relentless innovation drive their journeys. Each chapter provides a deep dive into critical aspects such as risk management, branding, philanthropy, and the power of media.

Learn how billionaires navigate the complex landscape of ethics, resilience, and global impact while planning their legacies for future generations. The book also sheds light on the scientific and technological advancements that are extending human lifespans and enhancing quality of life.

"The Legacy Code" is a captivating exploration of the principles and practices that define billionaire success. It offers valuable lessons and insights for aspiring leaders and anyone intrigued by the intersection of wealth, influence, and the pursuit of immortality.